History of Comic Books

David Smith, M.F.A., and
Jodene Smith, M.A.

Consultants

Timothy Rasinski, Ph.D.
Kent State University

Lori Oczkus, M.A.
Literacy Consultant

Publishing Credits

Rachelle Cracchiolo, M.S.Ed., *Publisher*
Conni Medina, M.A.Ed., *Managing Editor*
Dona Herweck Rice, *Series Developer*
Emily R. Smith, M.A.Ed., *Content Director*
Stephanie Bernard and Seth Rogers, *Editors*
Robin Erickson, *Multimedia Designer*

Image Credits: p.4 Old Paper Studios / Alamy; pp.6-7 ZUMA Press, Inc. / Alamy; p.9 Hulton Archive/Getty Images; p.10 Ronald Grant Archive / Alamy; p.12 Mario Tama/Getty Images; p.13 LOC [LC-DIG-ppmsca-17154]; p.14 Mim Friday / Alamy; p.15 FILM STILLS / Alamy; p.21 Barcroft Media /Barcoft Media via Getty Images; pp.22-23 Ted Pink / Alamy; pp.24-25 Atlaspix / Alamy; p.28 StampCollection / Alamy; p.33 Alan Levenson/The LIFE Images Collection/Getty Images; p.35 Warner Bros./AF archive / Alamy; p.37 Courtesy of Image Comics; pp.38-39 Marvel Studios/AF archive / Alamy; p.40 AF archive / Alamy; all other images from iStock and/or Shutterstock.

Library of Congress Cataloging-in-Publication Data

Names: Smith, David, 1973- author. | Smith, Jodene Lynn, author.
Title: History of comic books / David Smith and Jodene Smith.
Description: Huntington Beach, CA : Teacher Created Materials, 2016. | Includes index.
Identifiers: LCCN 2016012204 | ISBN 9781493835959 (pbk.)
Subjects: LCSH: Comic books, strips, etc.--History and criticism--Juvenile literature.
Classification: LCC PN6710 .S59 2016 | DDC 741.5/9--dc23
LC record available at http://lccn.loc.gov/2016012204

Teacher Created Materials
5301 Oceanus Drive
Huntington Beach, CA 92649-1030
http://www.tcmpub.com

ISBN 978-1-4938-3595-9

Printed by: 51497
Printed in: Taiwan

Table of Contents

The Beginning of Comics

Bam! Pow! Zing! What do these words make you think of? If you answered "a comic," then you already know a bit about comics. But there is so much more.

Political cartoons could be considered the first comics. They were used to make fun of political figures such as King George of England or President Abraham Lincoln. The cartoons also questioned authority. Artists drew these authority figures with weird bodies or exaggerated heads to make fun of them. King George was often drawn with a big behind. Imagine the popularity of that cartoon! Sometimes political cartoons were used to draw attention to injustices or to highlight current events. This style of comic still exists in newspaper editorial pages and magazines.

Color Is King

The Sunday comic pages began printing in color in the late 1800s. This was a big deal because the rest of the newspaper was black and white. Even movies were black and white back then!

Think Link

- Why are comics so much fun to read?
- Are comic books true art or just entertainment?
- Who is your favorite comic character? Why?

BAM

What Is a Comic?

Comics are stories told using pictures. The words being spoken are shown in word balloons. Clouds show what a person is thinking or dreaming.

Newspaper Heroes

In the early 1900s, the Sunday newspaper had an 8- to 16-page comic section! It was wrapped around the outside of the newspaper because it was everyone's favorite part.

The most famous comics from this time are *Gasoline Alley*, *Little Nemo in Slumberland*, and *Dick Tracy*. *Gasoline Alley* is filled with jokes about cars and small-town life. *Little Nemo* shows the adventures of Nemo in his dreams. *Dick Tracy* is about a detective. He faces off against all kinds of bad guys, such as Flattop Jones, who really has a flat head.

Make Me Laugh

Comic strips, also called *funnies*, usually had one to four pictures in a row. In the early 1900s, the strips were popular because they usually told jokes. Most comic strips told the entire joke in one strip. But some comic strips told stories that continued from day to day. Comics such as *Little Nemo in Slumberland* became story driven. They also began taking up more space in the comics section. Rather than only four panels, they took up a whole page! These longer and more story-driven comics are what evolved into full comic books.

The Cat Who Hates Mondays

Garfield is another world-famous comic strip. Garfield is a fat, lazy cat who complains to his owner, Jon, all day. He's known for loving lasagna and hating Mondays. This comic strip was created by Jim Davis in 1978 and continues today.

Peanuts crew

Quit While You're Ahead

Cartoonist Bill Watterson quit his beloved and enormously popular comic strip *Calvin and Hobbes* after ten years. He feared that his comic would become stale and lose its humor. Many people believe that if the strip had continued for many decades, it would perhaps have rivaled Charles M. Schulz's *Peanuts*.

Great Comic, Charlie Brown!

In time, *Peanuts* became one of the most popular and well-known comic strips. *Peanuts* is a comic strip about Charlie Brown, his friends, and his dog Snoopy. Charles M. Schulz created this four-panel comic in 1950. Schulz drew the *Peanuts* gang for over 50 years. *Peanuts* appeals to all ages because readers can identify with the different characters. Charlie Brown is the original "wimpy kid," but he has the coolest dog ever! The consistent four-panels drawn by Schulz made this format widely used by other comic-strip writers.

The Golden Age of Comics

Comics became so popular that they were too big for newspapers. They needed their own magazines, called comic books. At first, comic books were about humor, detectives, and romance. But everything changed with the success of Superman, who first appeared in *Action Comics* #1. Early issues of this series sold so well that he was awarded his own magazine, *Superman*, in 1939.

Birth of the Superhero

Jerry Siegel and Joe Shuster created *Superman*. During the Depression, they were looking for a hero to write positive stories about. They tried to get newspapers to print their comic strips. After a lot of rejection, they put their strips into a book and had it printed. The first successful comic book was born!

Superman was a smash success. Some early issues sold over a million copies. This led to new superhero comics. Others tried to duplicate the success of *Superman*. The heroes were always good and had incredible powers. These superpowers were the new story element that gave heroes the edge against evil.

Why The Golden Age?

This period is known as *The Golden Age* because it marks the first time these popular stories were told. Original comic books from this time are also the most valuable.

The Original Superpowers

Superman's superpowers have served as the basis for countless other superheroes. They include flight, heat vision, x-ray vision, super strength, super intelligence, the ability to deflect bullets, and super speed. He also has a secret identity, which becomes common for many other superheroes.

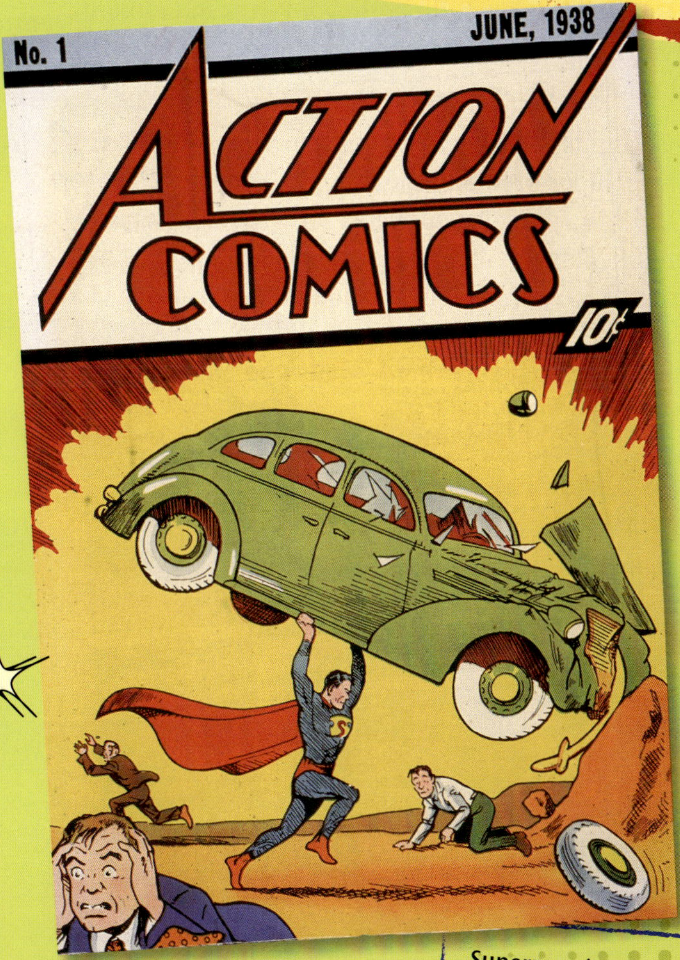

Superman is stronger and smarter than police and villains.

A Dark Spin

A year after the success of Superman, *Batman* was **published** by Detective Comics, also known as DC Comics™. Batman is a **vigilante** seeking his own kind of justice. Batman doesn't have any super powers and is fully human. But he does have his sharp wit and physical training. He also has unlimited financial resources. Batman is really Bruce Wayne, a billionaire who lives in Gotham City. Wayne uses his riches to pay for equipment to help him fight crime.

Batman fights for what is right. Sometimes, his way of doing this includes breaking the law. He wants revenge for the murder of his parents and wants all criminals to pay. Batman fights many evil characters. This level of darkness and desire to fight corruption in Gotham City has attracted readers to Batman for many years. It also created a new spin on the traditional superhero—one who has a dark side of his or her own.

Robin, Batman's sidekick

Sidekick

Dick Grayson is a boy who is saved by Batman. Grayson soon joins Batman as Robin the Boy Wonder, one of the most popular superhero sidekicks ever. But he wasn't the first—the Crimson Avenger's sidekick, Wing How, **debuted** in 1938. So did Fatman, Mister America's sidekick.

Love Interest?

Catwoman is a burglar in Gotham City who soon steals Batman's heart. His interest in her is evidence that he is a character with many **facets**, both light and dark. Many superhero characters that came since have followed suit.

Copycat?

At first, Captain America's shield was diamond shaped. But The Shield, another comic book hero of the time, had a badge-shaped design on his costume. The creators of The Shield wanted Captain America's shield changed. The creators of Captain America redesigned the shield to become the round one that we know today.

Comics Fight the Nazis

Comic books were used as part of the war effort during World War II. They helped to spread the message of the greatness of America. Material that spreads a message to help a cause is known as **propaganda**. Heroes that represented the United States were depicted. Real-world villains, such as German dictator Adolf Hitler, were also used. The armies of Germany, Japan, and Italy were shown as crazed thugs. This is now seen as an embarrassment to many comic book collectors today. The message to people was clear, though: Get in the war and be a real hero.

Captain America was born from this message. He is America in human form, created to fight against Nazi **atrocities**. Captain America is often shown fighting Hitler and the Nazis. There is even a famous illustration that shows him giving Hitler a punch on the jaw! He is **costumed** in the American flag and has a shield to protect himself. On a deeper level, he *is* the shield for all Americans.

Comics in the Field

Bill Mauldin was a soldier during World War II. He drew cartoons of the characters Willie and Joe as they faced the hardships of war. These comics were later published in the army newspaper *Stars and Stripes*. The hope was that they would encourage the troops to carry on.

Willie and Joe cartoon published April 4, 1941.

The Silver Age of Comics

"Good guy saves the day" remained the formula for comics for many years. After a while, the formula became too **predictable**. But, in the early 1960s, comics grew popular again. Creators such as Stan Lee brought new ideas. This period of comic history is known as *The Silver Age*. New life was breathed into existing heroes from the Golden Age, and many new heroes were added.

Hero Trouble

The Fantastic Four team does not always get along. Ben Grimm is easily **provoked** and fights with his teammates. Even nice guy, Mr. Fantastic, argues with his fiancée, Sue Storm. Johnny Storm, **aka** the Human Torch, **antagonizes** Ben and flies off the handle.

The Thing, aka Ben Grimm

A New Woman

The original superhero name for Sue Storm was The Invisible Girl. She kept the name until the 1980s, when it was updated to reflect social progress. Sue became The Invisible Woman.

Stan Lee Creates The Fantastic Four

Lee worked as a comic writer for more than a decade, but he was ready to quit. He hadn't had much success. His wife talked him into writing one last comic. She also encouraged him to change the comic formula. Stan wanted to write his characters with human flaws and problems. He gave it a try and created the comic *The Fantastic Four*.

Lee wrote about four ordinary people transformed by cosmic rays to gain superpowers. They worked together and alone to save the world. The new comic clobbered the competition! Before *The Fantastic Four*, heroes were practically perfect. This made them uninteresting. Lee's writing made comics more exciting.

The Fantastic Four was a financial success. Writers from that moment on were free to tell their own stories without following a formula.

Jack "The King" Kirby

Jack Kirby provided the visuals for most of the comics written by Stan Lee during the Silver Age. He drew the *Fantastic Four*, *X-Men*, *Hulk*, *Iron Man*, and *The Avengers*. He illustrated over one hundred *Fantastic Four* comics alone! Kirby drew the comics, designed what the characters looked like, and **influenced** story lines. Most of the popular heroes and villains of the time were designed by him.

Kirby's style is known for his **dynamic** action, bold character layout, and thick, simple lines. His art style soon became the "Marvel Style." Many artists have been influenced by his work.

Team Effort

A team of artists usually illustrates comic books. A penciler draws the comic pages with various pencils. An inker paints over the pencil lines in ink so the artwork stands out on printed newspaper. Letterers add the words, and colorists provide the color.

STOP! THINK...

"Kirby Krackles" are the way Jack Kirby drew energy blasts in comics. He used circular dabs of ink to create the look. They are still used today.

- Look at these red Kirby Krackles. What motion or message does each one convey to you?
- How would you show anger with your own Kirby Krackle? Excitement? Surprise?

Kirby Krackles

Character Shift

In 1962, Spider-Man made his debut in the comic *Amazing Fantasy* #15. At the time, it was a big risk. The worry was that readers would not like a nerdy, teenage superhero who lived with his old aunt. And a spider as a superhero? Nobody likes spiders.

Spider-Man became popular because of the character Peter Parker. Peter feels all the pain and hurt of ordinary people. That's because he is a normal person. Then, a radioactive spider bites him. This is what gives him superhero abilities. At first, Peter does not even want to be a superhero. But then, a thief kills his Uncle Ben. This makes Peter decide that he has a responsibility to protect others from harm.

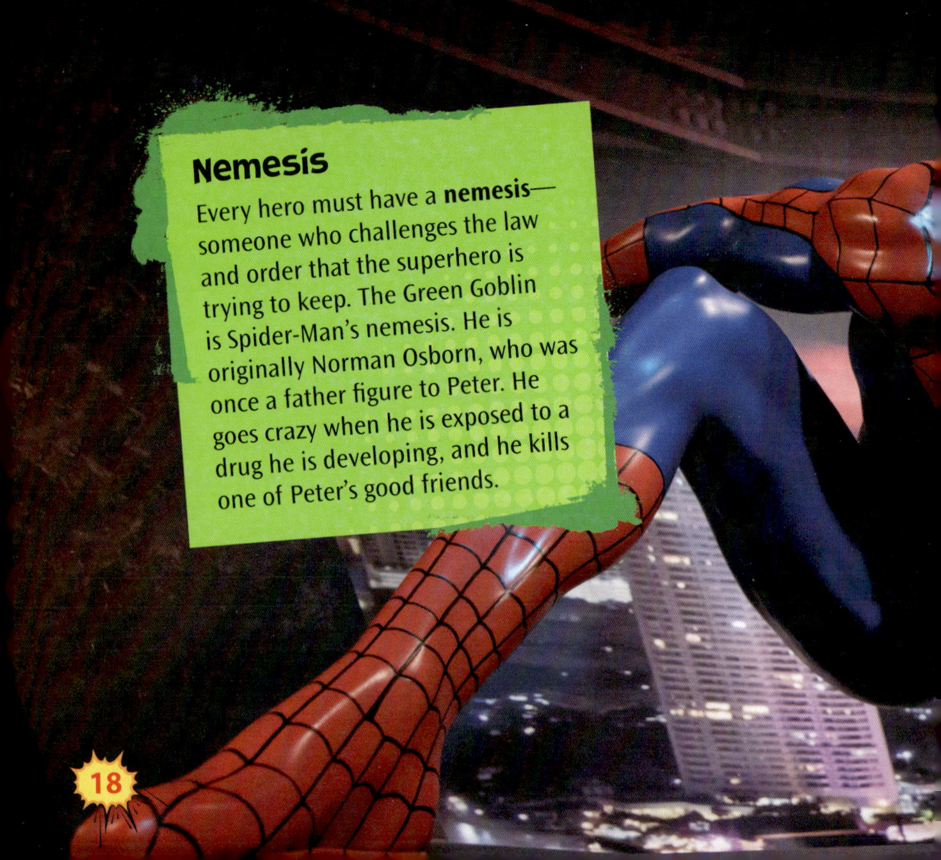

Nemesis

Every hero must have a **nemesis**—someone who challenges the law and order that the superhero is trying to keep. The Green Goblin is Spider-Man's nemesis. He is originally Norman Osborn, who was once a father figure to Peter. He goes crazy when he is exposed to a drug he is developing, and he kills one of Peter's good friends.

But Peter has all kinds of troubles. He always has to look after his Aunt May. Aunt May has poor health and does not have much money for medical help. Peter is not popular. He has a hard time with girls, especially the beautiful Gwen Stacy. Newspaper editor J. Jonah Jameson is always trying to blame Spider-Man for criminal acts. While Superman is a hero who is practically perfect and invulnerable, Peter Parker is a normal person who everyone can relate to.

Typical Teenage Boy

Peter has plenty of love interests, but he's not always savvy enough to realize how much someone likes him. He sometimes behaves awkwardly. This is normal, human, teenage behavior. It's part of why Peter Parker helped to create a new kind of superhero in the comic world.

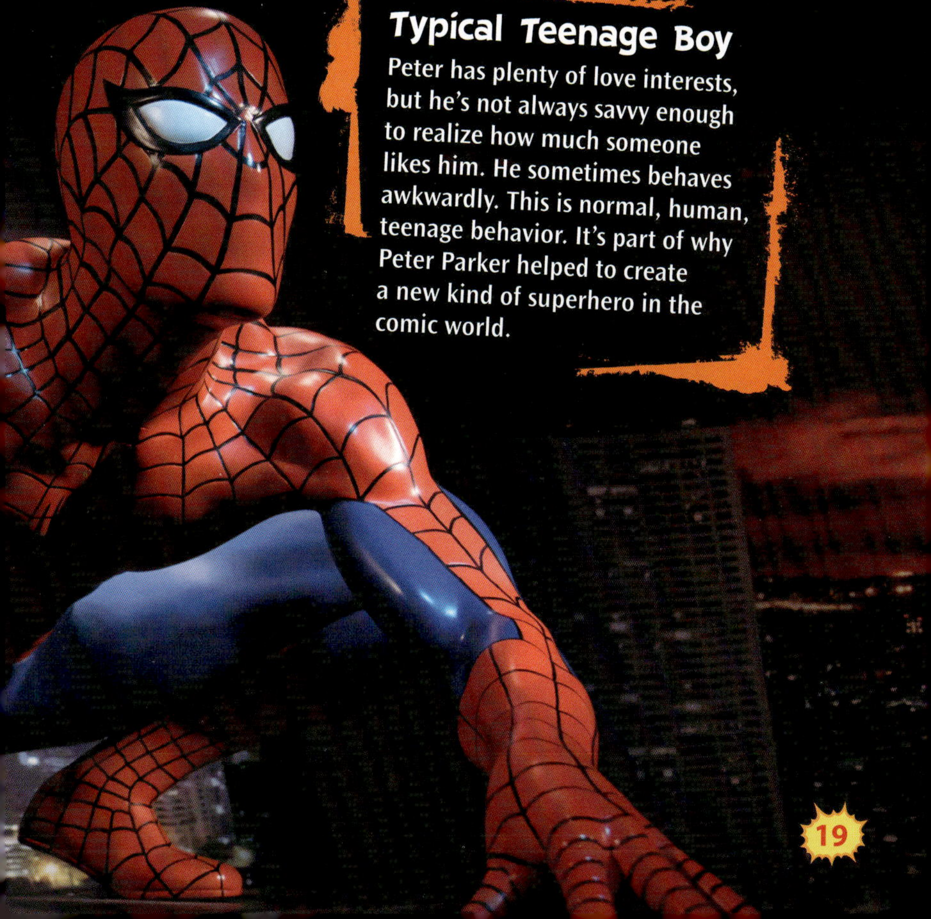

Crossing Worlds

In the Silver Age, Marvel Comics® was smashing the competition. Many Marvel characters had their own books. But fans loved it when heroes crossed over into other books. Thus, *The Avengers* was born. The Avengers is a team of heroes. They come together to face even bigger threats than each one faces alone. The first lineup was the Hulk, Iron Man, Thor, Ant-Man, and the Wasp. In the fourth issue, Captain America joins the team. He has been leading newer Avengers teams ever since.

Big Movie Business!

The movie world has capitalized on many individual character's worlds. But it has also included the crossover worlds of many combined characters. Fans flock to films that showcase these worlds coming together in new and exciting ways.

The Avengers aren't always buddies, though. There is a lot of fighting among themselves. The Hulk rarely gets along with anybody. Captain America is always having fights with Tony Stark (Iron Man) and Hawkeye about doing the right thing.

One of the Avengers' biggest threats is Kang the Conqueror. Kang first appears in the *Fantastic Four* but soon becomes a **reoccurring** villain for the Avengers. Kang is a time traveler who rules over ancient Egypt for a time before being defeated by the Fantastic Four. Kang escapes and has been wreaking havoc ever since.

Which Team?

There have been many Avengers teams, including The West Coast Avengers, The New Avengers, and even The Dark Avengers. Many Marvel characters have become part of the Avengers, including members of the Fantastic Four.

DIG DEEPER!

How to Read and Collect Comic Books

There are different opinions on how to read and collect comics books. Here are a few tips to keep in mind.

Bag and Board

Comic books are usually kept in plastic bags with cardboard backs to keep them safe. But if you bag and board your comics, it takes up more room in your comic box. Some readers don't use these and just carefully put their comics in a box.

Extra Copies?

Some collectors buy two copies of a comic, one to read and one to put away as an investment. This keeps one copy in **mint condition**. Also, sometimes comics have different versions of the same issue. For example, the same story can have several different covers. It can be very expensive to buy these **variants**, but they are usually more valuable in the long run. Some collectors just buy one copy of a comic that they actually want to read. This frees up their money for more, and different, comics.

Pulling Titles

Many comic book stores have a "pull" system. This involves making a list of comics you want to read. Then, the store will set aside new issues for you before they sell out. This can be a nice convenience, but keep in mind that you are then obligated to buy the pulled issues. New comics come out on Wednesdays. Many collectors enjoy showing up to the store once a week to see what is new, even if they already have a pull list.

Read or Collect?

Collecting comics can be expensive, and most of the time, it is not worth the investment. Comic-book paper **deteriorates** over time unless you seal it in plastic—but what would be the fun in that? It may be better to simply buy and read your favorite comics and buy extra copies of your favorite series or special stories as investments.

Punk Rock 80s

The 1980s were influenced by punk rock culture. But in the '80s, comics were getting predictable. Most of the characters had not aged much or changed in 20 years. Some big changes were about to shake things up!

A Dark Turn

Frank Miller created a special series about Batman called *The Dark Knight Returns*. Miller was a fan of Batman, but he was dissatisfied to find the character had changed very little in 50 years. Miller wanted something new, so in his comic, Batman has aged. This brings a new story to the mix because Batman has to rely on his wits and experience more than his **brawn**.

Miller's comic is darker and more violent than previous Batman comics. It is aimed at an older audience—adults who loved Batman as kids. Before Miller's comic, many people saw Batman as clean-cut and goofy with funny sound effects. Now, Batman is serious. The story has more mature themes. *The Dark Knight Returns* was later made into a **graphic novel**, which helped comics first become recognized as serious literature.

Like Stan Lee, Frank Miller changed the way we read and think about comics. Today, comics express great freedom of voice. They can have their own structure, ideas, and stories.

Another World

Frank Miller made many changes to the story line in his special series. So many things are different that *The Dark Knight Returns* is not considered part of the DC Universe.

Woman Power

In Miller's *The Dark Knight Returns,* he wrote in a new Robin named Carrie Kelley. That's right—a female Robin. The male Robin is presumed dead, and Batman is remorseful for it.

Gen X Influence

During the '80s, *The X-Men* grew in popularity. It tells the story of teenage mutants. They are rejected and feared because they are different. These mutants might have special powers, but normal people still bully them. They are outcasts who want dignity and respect.

During this same time, the character Wolverine hit stardom. Wolverine plays by his own rules and is almost as bad as he is good. The idea of an **antihero** was a hit with teens.

The two great leaders of the X-Men world were modeled after acclaimed real-world leaders of the 1960s, and the characters were meant to offer commentary on the various social movements for civil rights. Professor X is the teacher and leader of the X-Men. He feels that mutants could better help humans. Professor X mirrors the leadership of Dr. Martin Luther King Jr. His counterpart and friend is Magneto. Magneto teaches that mutants should fight against prejudices and inequality. He is, in some ways, based on Malcolm X.

Social Commentary

Comic books have always shed light on political and social issues of their times. Even humorous newspaper comic strips offer comment on issues. And of course, the main job of editorial cartoons (found in newspapers and magazines) is to do exactly that.

"And tell him I hate it when he uses the dog to communicate!"

Antiheroes such as Wolverine have become very popular.

Character Evolution

Over time, comic-book heroes have evolved. They show deeper layers of human psychology and face more-complex challenges. Their special abilities may be as unworldly as the original superheroes, but they have become increasingly human, and flawed, at the same time.

DIG DEEPER!

The Rise of Indie Comics

The two biggest publishers of comics are Marvel and DC Comics. There have always been other comic book publishers, though. In the 1980s, many new comics were created. They were published by smaller companies. These independent companies are often called **indie publishers**.

Dark Horse Comics and Image Comics are two large independent publishers. Dark Horse published titles such as *The Mask* and *Hellboy*. They also make films and TV shows.

Image Comics was formed by comic-book celebrities that left Marvel. They wanted to create their own heroes and have creative control over their comics. Image features many comics that don't fit into the superhero mold. *The Walking Dead* is one of their most popular.

Archie Comics

Two comic books that have been around for years are *Archie* and *Jughead*. In fact, *Archie* has been around since 1942. They are published by Archie Comics. Can they be considered indie successes? Absolutely! They have existed and remained popular for decades outside the mainstream publishers.

Independent Successes

These comics published by independent companies have been highly successful.

- *Teenage Mutant Ninja Turtles* published by Mirage Studios
- *The Mask* published by Dark Horse
- *Next Men* published by Dark Horse
- *Usagi Yojimbo* published by Dark Horse
- *Cerebus* published by Aardvark-Vanaheim
- *Spawn* published by Image Comics

The Death of Comics?

The comic **industry** enjoyed many years of success. But things changed in the 1990s. People were choosing movies, television, and video games for entertainment. Fewer and fewer comics were being bought.

The Collecting Bulge

Collecting comics was still popular in the early '90s, though. Comic sales **inflated**, and Marvel and DC Comics expanded. The publishers hired many people who didn't directly make the comics. In the 1960s, Stan Lee wrote, edited, and oversaw production. He earned the nickname Stan "The Man" Lee. By the '90s, it took many people to do what Lee had done before. All those extra people had to be paid.

Publishers tried to increase sales with clever schemes. Special covers were designed with foil and **holograms**. Also, many series were restarted with new number 1 issues. First-issue comics are collectible, and this technique helped to drive up sales. Finally, the same comic was printed with different cover art, which made collectors want to buy them all.

These tricks helped increase sales for a little while. But soon, collectors felt taken advantage of. They could not keep buying all the special issues. The increased sales were like a balloon, and that balloon eventually burst.

The world of comics began to crash.

Collector Woes

Many collectors stopped reading comics. They only bought the books as collectibles or for the trading cards or toys. Because of this, writers were not likely to write good stories, and poor storytelling became more common.

All-Time Record Comic Book Sales			
Title	**Issue Date**	**Cover Price**	**Sold For**
Action Comics #1	Jun. 1938	$0.10	$3,207,852.00
Amazing Fantasy #15	Aug. 1962	$0.12	$1,100,000.00
Detective Comics #27	May 1939	$0.10	$1,075,000.00
Batman #1	Spring 1940	$0.10	$567,625.00
X-Men #1	Sept. 1963	$0.12	$492,937.00
Flash Comics #1	Jan. 1940	$0.10	$450,000.00
Tales of Suspense #39	Mar. 1963	$0.12	$375,000.00
Marvel Comics #1	Oct. 1939	$0.10	$350,000.00
Captain America Comics #1	Mar. 1941	$0.10	$343,057.00
Incredible Hulk #1	May 1962	$0.12	$326,000.00

Source: http://itsalljustcomics.com/all-time-record-comic-book-sales/

Pre-bagged?

Many comics in the '90s were sealed in plastic bags. The bags often included some trading cards. This increased the price. It also kept readers from previewing the comics before buying them.

DIG DEEPER!

Comic Book Celebrities

Sales were driven by artistic style in the early '90s. This made the artists into superstars. Several superstar artists wanted control over their comics. They left Marvel and formed their own studios. Together, the studios formed a publishing company. They called it Image Comics.

Celebrity Artist	Original Work at Marvel
Todd McFarlane	**Spider-Man, Hulk**
Rob Liefeld	**X-Force, Cable, Deadpool**
Jim Lee	**X-Men**
Erik Larsen	**Spider-Man**
Marc Silvestri	**X-Men, Wolverine**

Deadpool and Cable Live!

Rob Liefeld rose quickly into comic stardom when he worked at Marvel. He cocreated Cable and Deadpool. These two characters are still very popular. To this day, Marvel markets them heavily.

New Studio	New Comic Title
Todd McFarlane Productions	*Spawn*
Extreme Studios	*Youngblood*
Wildstorm Productions	*WildC.A.T.S.*
Highbrow Entertainment	*The Savage Dragon*
Top Cow Entertainment	*Cyber Force*

The Death of Superman

Just before the comic book crash, Superman fought his most dangerous **foe**, Doomsday. This led to his death in the comic *Superman* #75 (1992). Doomsday is practically indestructible. He causes plenty of damage to Metropolis. Superman, Supergirl, and the Justice League of America team up to fight him. Lex Luthor is on the scene to disrupt and sabotage Superman's efforts. In the end, Superman gives his life to end Doomsday's. Superman's love, Lois Lane, cradles him in her arms as he dies.

This issue of *Superman* sold over 2.5 million copies. That was a huge boost in the number of readers. The death of Superman was reported in newspapers and on television. It was talked about for a long time. After Superman's death, DC Comics quickly introduced four new comics. They were spin-offs of Superman. The result was Superman's return about a year later.

Many readers were disappointed with DC Comics for bringing Superman back so quickly. Interest in the comic waned. Since the death of Superman, readers don't take the death of popular heroes seriously. They just assume they will return when sales are down.

THINK LINK

- Why is Superman so important to comics?
- In your opinion, was the death of Superman motivated by the story or money?
- Why might Superman never really die?

The Comic Book Crash

Many point to the death of Superman as the cause of the comic book crash. Collectors bought multiple copies of that issue. They were hoping to sell the copies for a profit. In fact, many people who didn't even read comics bought copies, hoping the value would increase. And some people knew that **rare** copies of the first-ever Superman comic have been sold for millions! They hoped for the same with *Superman* #75. But the problem is that the price usually only goes up when the comic is rare, and *Superman* #75 is not rare. In fact, it is the most printed comic ever. When the value of the comic didn't rise, collectors became frustrated.

Rise of the Graphic Novel

The graphic novel as a literary form has been on the rise while comic interest has waned. Some graphic novels are collections of comics. Others tell complete stories on their own. Many graphic novels have won literary awards and have been turned into popular movies and plays.

Comics to Toys

Todd McFarlane was one of the most popular artists. He moved away from drawing comics and started a toy company. The company creates popular action figures based on comic books and movies.

Readers lost interest in comics. They felt that comics had become less about the story and more about marketing. Comics also were not being released regularly due to delays and missed deadlines. This caused the stories to progress at painfully slow rates.

Indie for the Win!

Even after the crash, independent comics are still doing well. Their creators love their work and love telling stories. Image Comics is a huge supporter of these creator-owned comics, such as *Saga* and *The Walking Dead*.

Comic Books Are Forever

The comic book crash couldn't keep comics down for long. Comic books continue to be printed. Their stories have been shaped to different **media**, too.

Comic sales eventually dropped to about a tenth of what they were in the '90s. Some consider the industry to be barely surviving. But the die-hard readers and collectors continue to buy. And independent comics continue to tell their stories.

TV Shows

Many popular comic books have been adapted into successful TV shows over the years. One popular comic book show is *The Incredible Hulk* (1978–82). The show is dramatic and moody. In it, David Banner exposes himself to radiation. This transforms him into the Hulk. He becomes the Hulk whenever he is angry. The show often **depicts** Banner running from authorities. He is desperately trying to cure his condition.

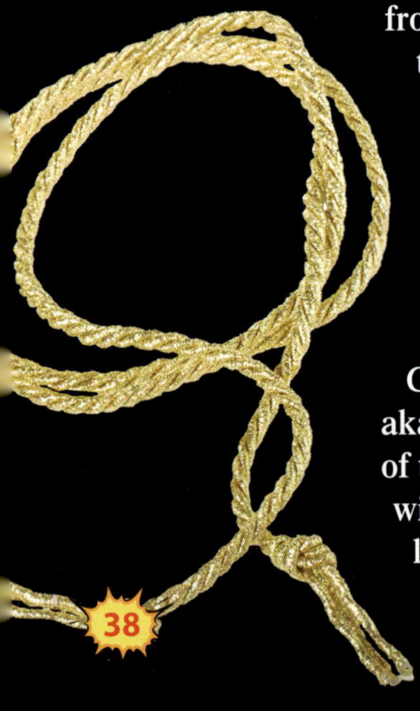

Another notable show made from comics is *Wonder Woman* (1975–79). The show is full of action and has a fantasy focus. Its first airing was hugely popular with both boys and girls. Much like Captain America, Wonder Woman, aka Diana Prince, is dressed in the colors of the American flag. She is equipped with bulletproof bracelets and a golden lasso. She even has an invisible jet.

DC on TV

Smallville, *Arrow*, *Gotham*, *The Flash*, and *Supergirl* are just a few shows that come directly from the DC world.

X-Men: The Animated Series

In the '90s, an animated show was made about the X-Men. It helped boost the popularity of the comic.

Movies

Comic book movies became more popular with the 1978 movie *Superman*. Though this was the first Superman movie to gain major popularity, there have been Superman movies for a long time—almost since Superman first appeared in the pages of a comic book! There are sure to be many more Superman movies in the future.

Comic Movie Reboots

Several popular comics have made their way into television and film—many, many times. These are some of the most popular series to reboot:

- Superman
- Spider-Man
- The Avengers
- Batman
- Fantastic Four
- X-Men

Comics have flooded movie theatres for decades. But now their popularity is on the rise, and there is no sign of it letting up. From Superman to the X-Men to the Avengers, many kids today have been exposed to comics through movies. You can usually expect a few comic-book movies each year.

Is this a coincidence? Well, not really. The explosion of comic book movies can be explained. Both Marvel and DC are now owned by large media corporations. Time Warner owns DC, and Disney owns Marvel. These companies are in the business of making big entertainment.

Stan Lee Cameo

Stan Lee has had a **cameo** role in most Marvel movies. It has become a tradition—so be sure to look for him!

Stan Lee

Modern-Day Mythology

Comics tell stories filled with heroes and god-like characters. They express our need for justice, for survival, and to fight against evil. Visual stories, such as comics, can be shared in any country. The images speak in ways beyond what words can do.

Comics also bring us adventure, mystery, and action. These are things that many of us lack in our safe, modern lives. Comics are forms of fantasy fiction and can take our imaginations further than what we experience in our everyday lives. Comics also create discussion and fellowship among fans and friends. They can even teach us about ourselves.

Telling stories through pictures helps us communicate when words cannot. We crave heroes who mirror our convictions and fight for what is right. Comics are exciting and thoughtful. They offer a modern-day **mythology** for the masses. This is why comics have lasted for so many years.

Not So Super!

Today, many popular comics do not include superheroes. Instead, the central figure is someone who digs into his or her human abilities to resolve whatever conflict arises. Those conflicts may be tragedies, personal turmoil, or the forces of evil. Some examples of these modern comic series include *The Walking Dead*, *Saga*, and *Star Wars*.

Glossary

aka—abbreviation for also known as

antagonizes—makes mad or upset

antihero—a character who doesn't have the usual good qualities of a hero

atrocities—cruel or terrible acts

brawn—strength

cameo—a short appearance

costumed—wearing a special outfit or costume, usually representing a character or theme

debuted—first appeared

depicts—tells or shows

deteriorates (dih-TEER-ee-uhr-ayts)—falls apart; dissolves

dynamic—exciting

facets—parts of something

foe—an enemy

graphic novel—a story of book length told in comic form

holograms—flat images that appear to be three dimensional

indie publishers—smaller publishing companies independent of a large company

industry—business

inflated—blown up; gotten bigger

influenced—made an impact

media—methods for sharing news, such as television, radio, and magazines

mint condition—perfect; not damaged or showing any signs of use

mythology—stories meant to explain things, often in magical or unscientific ways

nemesis—worst enemy

predictable—behaving in a way that is expected

propaganda—messages spread to support a cause

provoked—made mad

published—printed book, magazine, or newspaper

rare—not common; hard to find

reoccurring—happening often and in the same way

variants—different details; versions

vigilante (vij-ih-LAN-tee)—a person who is not part of the standard legal system who punishes criminals on his or her own

Index

Check It Out!

Books

Bendis, Brian Michael, Sara Pichelli, Chris Samnee, and David Marquez. 2015. *Miles Morales: Ultimate Spider-Man Collection Book 1*. Marvel.

Gaiman, Neil. 2008. *Coraline: The Graphic Novel*. Harper Collins.

Goulart, Ron. 2000. *Comic Book Culture: An Illustrated History*. Collectors Press.

Lee, Stan, and Jack Kirby. 2015. *Marvel Masterworks: Fantastic Four, Vol. 1*. Marvel.

Lee, Stan, and Jack Kirby. 2015. *Marvel Masterworks: The Amazing Spider-Man, Vol. 1*. Marvel.

Miller, Frank. 2016. *Batman: The Dark Knight Returns 30th Anniversary Edition*. DC Comics.

Schumer, Arlen. 2014. *The Silver Age of Comic Book Art*. Archway Publishing.

Videos

Zakarin, Scott. 2002. *Stan Lee's Mutants, Monsters & Marvels: Creating Spider-Man and Here Come the Heroes*. Sony Pictures/Creative Light, DVD.

Websites

Marvel. http://www.marvel.com/

DC Comics. http://www.dccomics.com/

Comic Book Resources. http://www.comicbookresources.com/

Try It!

Imagine that you're an up-and-coming comic book artist. You've just been offered a job with a major comic book publisher to create a brand new comic. POW! You should get to work. You've got some decisions to make:

- Draw a picture or write a description of the character your comic will be about.
- Decide what kinds of special talents or powers your character will have.
- Decide what sort of evil villain, mutant, or enemy your character might be up against.
- Plan some of the things you'll need to draw and write your comic book (a desk, sketching paper, colored pencils, a storyboard to map out the plot, and so on).
- Think about the backstory for your character. Is it a normal person with amazing powers? Is it a funny, quirky animal who gets into all sorts of trouble?

About the Authors

David Smith worked in comics in the early '90s as a colorist for Extreme Studios, employed by comic celebrity Rob Liefeld. He then went on to color comics independently for Marvel and DC. He currently teaches digital arts at the Fashion Institute of Design and Merchandising, and he creates his own independent comics.

Jodene Smith has been in education for over 25 years. She is currently a teacher in the ABC Unified School District. She has authored, edited, or managed hundreds of publications for teachers and students.

The Smiths have two children and live in Southern California.